# HOW TO LIVE LIKE

# A SAMURAI WARRIOR

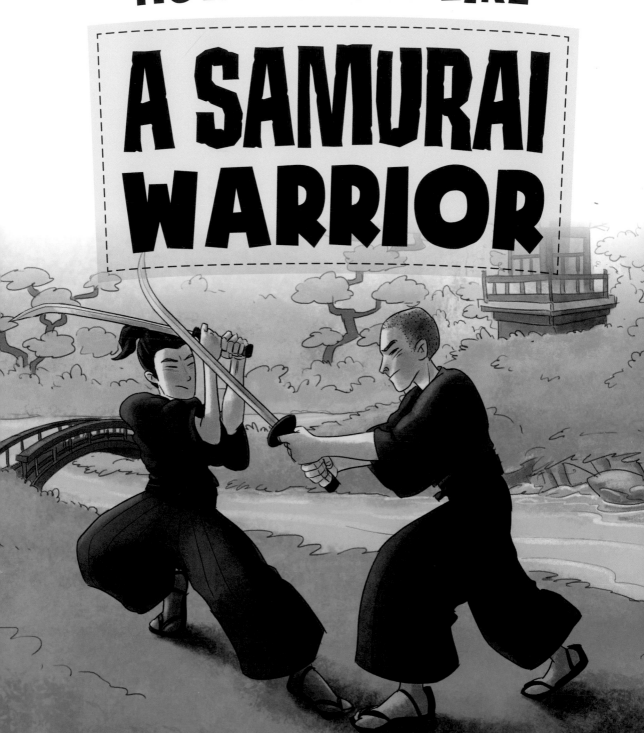

Thanks to the creative team:
Senior Editor: Alice Peebles
Consultant: John Haywood
Fact checking: Kate Mitchell
Design: www.collaborate.agency

Hungry Tomato™
A division of Lerner Publishing Group, Inc.
241 First Avenue North
Minneapolis, MN 55401 USA

For reading levels and more information, look up
this title at www.lernerbooks.com.

Main body text set in Century Gothic Regular 10/13.
Typeface provided by Monotype Typography.

**Library of Congress Cataloging-in-Publication Data**

The Cataloging-in-Publication Data for
*How to Live Like a Samurai Warrior*
is on file at the Library of Congress.
ISBN 978-1-5124-0630-6 (lib. bdg.)
ISBN 978-1-5124-1163-8 (pbk.)
ISBN 978-1-5124-0917-8 (EB pdf)

Manufactured in the United States of America
1 – VP – 7/15/16

# HOW TO LIVE LIKE A SAMURAI WARRIOR

by John Farndon

Illustrated by Amerigo Pinelli

HUNGRY TOMATO.

# contents

The Great Warlords...................................................6

Life in a Samurai Castle...........................................8

Samurai School.......................................................10

The Way of the Warrior.......................................... 12

Samurai Swords......................................................14

The Art of the Bow................................................ 16

Fighting Hand-to-Hand........................................... 18

Samurai with Guns.................................................20

Splendid Armor......................................................22

The Shadow Warriors .............................................24

Into Battle.............................................................26

The Final Victory ...................................................28

Ten Shocking Samurai Facts....................................30

Glossary................................................................ 31

Index....................................................................32

# The Great Warlords

It's 1546 and you've landed in Japan. My name is Takeshi and I'm going to be a samurai, like my father and his father before him. It's the same for everyone in Japan—you do what your dad does. Everyone has a place. At the very top is the emperor, and then come warrior lords, or shogun and daimyo. Every daimyo has his personal army, and in spring, he goes on a procession through all his lands with his army—so everyone knows how powerful he is. We kids just stare as they move by, their armor glinting in the sun, and banners waving.

Right in the middle of the procession is the daimyo himself, carried in a luxurious canopied litter (like a cabin). He has his own personal guard of samurai around him. That's where I'll be some day!

Russia

China

Japan

## Know Your Place

Here's a diagram of everyone's place in Japan in the sixteenth century. No one has any choice; that's just how it is. The emperor, shogun, and daimyo are at the top. We samurai are just below. Then come the farmers and peasants, and at the bottom are merchants and artisans.

Emperor

Shogun

Daimyo

Samurai

Farmers and Peasants

Merchants and Artisans

The daimyo in a procession through his lands

## The First Shogun

In Japan, we have an emperor, but it's a warrior leader, or shogun, who really runs the country. It's been that way since Minamoto Yoritomo became the first shogun in 1192. And every shogun needs samurai to keep things under control!

# Life in a Samurai Castle

I have come to live in a castle to do my training. There are thousands of samurai castles in Japan, but the biggest of all is Himeji Castle. It is known as White Heron castle, because its white wooden walls and winged roofs look like herons taking flight! Castles are the centers of life in Japan, and towns are built around them. A daimyo must make his castle as magnificent as possible, just so you know how powerful and elegant he is. My daimyo made Himeji the best castle of all.

This picture shows Himeji Castle as it was rebuilt soon after Takeshi lived here. It looks like a house, and is luxurious inside, with polished wood floors, painted silk screens, and cushions. But it's surrounded by moats and built on a high stone platform with sloping sides, so it is tough to attack.

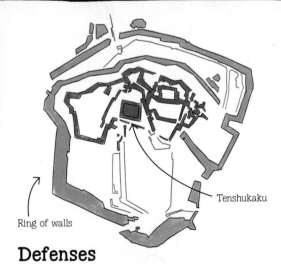

Tenshukaku

Ring of walls

## Defenses

Beyond the central tower or *tenshukaku*, there is a ring of walls which act as first defenses against an attack.

## Tea Ceremony

A samurai must drink tea properly. It takes years to learn the correct way. It's very calm and quiet. We sit on straw mats. First the host prepares tea in a bowl. Then each guest takes just three sips. He wipes the bowl and passes it on. The ceremony can go on for hours.

# samurai school

I've been away from home at samurai school since I was five. It's a hard life. We must be clean and polite at all times. We must go to sleep early and wake up early. If I doze off, the master will hit me hard with the back of his sword. And we must learn to be tough. We must never, ever cry or complain. Sometimes, the master makes me walk barefoot in the snow all the way to the river and back. And once I had to sit for three hours under an icy waterfall—*brrr*! But it's all part of the training.

## Writing, Not Fighting

Training to be a samurai isn't just about fighting skills. We must learn to read and write. First of all, there are two letter systems: *hiragana* for letters to friends and *katakana* for official letters. Then there are also thousands of different *kanji* symbols or "characters," each meaning something different! And I must practice shaping the letters with a brush pen until they are totally beautiful. This is called calligraphy. Oh, and we learn to write poetry, too. Skill in poetry is just as important to a samurai as skill with sword. I write a short poem called a *waka* every day.

We learn how to fight with wooden swords called *bokken*. They are not toys and are shaped like real swords. You can kill someone with a bokken! We have to practice seriously every day and learn all the right moves. It's vital to hold the *kissaki* (tip) pointing up.

# The Way of the Warrior

Being a samurai isn't just about learning skills, such as fighting and writing. It must be your whole life. Another word for samurai is *busho*, and we have to learn *bushido*. This means "the way of the warrior." It is a code that tells you how to live your life virtuously, how to tell right from wrong, and how to be brave. Above all it tells you how to live and die honorably. Not every samurai follows the same bushido. Some don't bother with all parts of the code. But to me, they are not proper samurai!

All samurai learn *The Tale of the Heike*. This is the great story of the battles between the Taira and Minamoto families to control Japan in the twelfth century. It's an exciting adventure in which the great samurai Minamoto no Yoshinaka battles the evil Taira no Kiyomori. But it also teaches us two Buddhist truths: *mujo* and *karma*. Mujo says that nothing lasts for long. Karma tells you that everything you do comes back to you later!

In the nineteenth century, a historian summarized the key virtues of the samurai:

**Rectitude:** Deciding calmly and quickly what to do and when

**Courage:** Being brave enough to do what is right

**Mercy:** The greatest quality a warrior or ruler needs

**Politeness:** Considering the feelings of others

**Honesty:** Shunning riches and waste

**Honor:** Behaving with true dignity at all times

**Loyalty:** Staying true to your leaders, family, and friends

**Character:** Being always in control of yourself

## Wise Master

When you're training as a samurai, the most important person in your life is your *sensei*—your teacher. The older he is, the more likely he is to be wise in the way of the warrior. It takes a lifetime to learn even a fraction of what there is to know.

# samurai swords

A samurai is above all a swordsman. So I practise *kenjutsu*, the art of swordsmanship, many hours a day. I got my first sword at the age of thirteen, and I will sleep with a sword under my pillow for the rest of my life. A samurai's sword is not just a weapon. It is everything we stand for. Some say our soul lives in our sword. Actually, we have two swords, a long curved *katana* and a short *wakizashi*. Together they are called the *daisho*, but we only fight with one at a time.

## Making a Sword

Making a samurai sword takes many months. First, the sword maker forms a rough flexible core or *shingane* of low carbon steel. On this he carefully builds up thousands of layers of *tamahagane* or high carbon steel, folding it over and over for a sharp cutting edge. Everyone wants the swordsmith Muramasa Senji's blades—they are so sharp they are said to be evil.

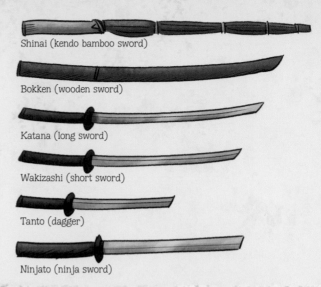

Shinai (kendo bamboo sword)

Bokken (wooden sword)

Katana (long sword)

Wakizashi (short sword)

Tanto (dagger)

Ninjato (ninja sword)

To use a katana properly, you must learn the *kamae*—different ways to stand and hold the sword.

*Hasso no kamae* is ready for attack from any angle

*Ko gasumi* defends against attacks to the head

*Gedan no kamae* invites an attack

*Jodan no kame* is when you're ready to strike

# The Art of the Bow

Not so long ago, a bow and arrow was the samurai's main weapon. Even now, we must still learn *kyujutsu*, the art of the bow. We use the world's biggest bow, called a *yumi*. It's more than 6.5 feet (2 meters) long! What's more, we have to fire it from a galloping horse. That's really difficult—and dangerous. Just think. You have to let go of the reins completely. Then you pull an arrow from your quiver. Set the arrow on the bow string. Draw the string back as you raise the bow. Take aim and finally let the arrow fly. And then do it all again…while trying to stay on the horse!

## Whirling Pole

The *naginata* was a long pole with a blade which samurai whirled about with amazing skill. Female samurai especially used a naginata. Some samurai could stop a hail of arrows by whirling their naginata.

The feats of samurai archers are legendary. In a special challenge, the samurai Nasu Yoichi hit a fan that was hung on a mast far away, while riding through the water. And Minamoto Tametomo sank a ship just by hitting it below the waterline.

The greatest female samurai, or *onna-bugeisha*, was Tomoe Gozen, the Lady Tomoe. She was a brilliant archer and rider, and was deadly with a sword, too. She was a hero in the Battle of Awazu in 1184, fighting alongside her husband, the legendary samurai Yoshinaka.

# Fighting
## Hand-to-Hand

Sometimes, you may be caught by surprise
and deprived of all your weapons. Or you
may be forced to fight so close that you
cannot wield your sword. So a samurai
must learn the art of *jujutsu,* fighting
bare-handed. Jujutsu means the "gentle
art" and the idea is to use your opponent's
force rather than your own to defeat him.
We learn not to strike our foe, but instead
throw him, stop him moving, or choke him.
By doing that, one man may fight off three.
We didn't call it jujutsu when I was training.
Jujutsu's a new word. We just learned it as
part of fighting skills called *Takenouchi-ryu.*

## Big Fans

It's hot in Japan in
summer, but a samurai
with a fan may not be just
keeping cool! Most samurai
carry a folding metal fan
called a *tessen.* If you're
visiting someone without
your sword, a tessen makes
a good weapon—and if
you're skilled you can use
it to deflect arrows. And
a big *gumbai* fan makes a
good shield. Very cool.

The secret of jujutsu is *haragei* or willpower, not strong muscles. Muscle power (*chikara*) weakens as you get older, but haragei gets stronger. That's why an old man can use jujutsu to defeat young warriors.

# Samurai with Guns

Just a few years after I was born, we discovered a weapon so deadly
that all our old skills may soon be useless—the gun. Guns are frightening!
They use gunpowder to fire a metal ball at such high speeds it can
kill a man from far away. Arrows are still much easier to use and more
accurate. But already some samurai have guns called *tanegashima*.
Who knows what guns may be able to do one day?
I must get hold of one and learn to use it.

## Tanegashima

The name Tanegashima comes from a Japanese island where a Portuguese pirate ship sheltered from a storm in 1543. The lord of Tanegashima got his swordsmith to copy two matchlock rifles he bought from the pirates. Soon many different kinds of gun were being made all over Japan.

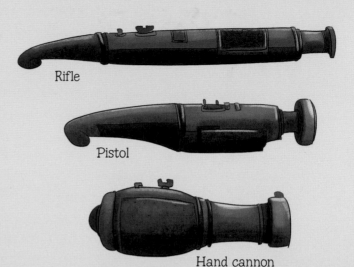

Rifle

Pistol

Hand cannon

## Fiery Rain

Flaming arrows or *bo-hiya* are fired at the enemy to cause confusion or set buildings alight. We always used to fire bo-hiya with a bow. But now some samurai are learning to fire them from guns. Bo-hiya fired from ranks of soldiers with guns may fall like fiery rain upon the enemy.

## The End of Swords

The Battle of Nagashino in 1575 ended the days when swords ruled. I was fighting there for the mighty daimyo Takeda Katsuyori. With swords, we had been all-powerful. But in that battle, our forces were utterly destroyed by just three thousand gunners hidden behind a bank and firing volleys at us, one thousand shots at a time. Slaughter!

# Splendid Armor

I have passed through many years of training, and I have come of age. My head has been partly shaved on top and I have a short tail at the back, so that I can wear a helmet without overheating. And now I have my first suit of armor! A samurai's armor is very tough and will protect me well in battle. But it is also very light and folds easily into a box for carrying on journeys. It is enameled in bright colors to protect it from the weather. So I think I look magnificent!

Every part of a samurai's armor has a name, such as the *haidate* that protect the thighs and the *kote* that cover the arms. The main parts are made from iron scales sewn together and attached to a leather backing. That makes it easy for me to move about and jump on and off a horse in my armor. If parts of the armor are damaged, or the cords cut, they are easily replaced. But the best bit for me is my spectacular helmet with its horns and wide neck protector.

## Putting on Armor

Doing this correctly is quite a task!

**1** First I put on a loose kimono, baggy pants, and thigh and shin guards to protect my legs.

**2** I attach the *haidate* over my thighs and my *yugake* (under-gloves) which then need to be tied to my sleeves.

**3** I tie the parts of the *kote* over each of my arms and the *sode* to protect my shoulders.

**4** Then I pull the *do* over my head to protect my upper body and tie the *kusazuri* (belt of protective plates) around my waist.

**5** The last thing I put on is my helmet.

**Katana:**
long sword

**Tekko:**
hand guard

**Do:**
breast plate

**Haidate:**
thigh protector

**Tabi:**
traditional sock

**Kabuto:**
helmet

**Sode:**
shoulder protector

**Kote:**
arm guard

**Wakizashi:**
short sword

**Suneate:**
shin guard

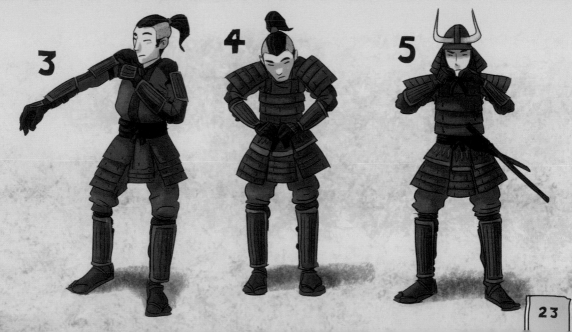

3

4

5

# The Shadow Warriors

We samurai always meet our enemies face to face in open combat. Not the sneaky, shameless ninja, though! Ninja are sent by daimyo to spy on their enemies or secretly sabotage them. Worst of all, ninja creep in at night and assassinate you in your bed. And they are very good at it! I hate them. People have spread silly tales that they can make themselves invisible, or even fly. That's not true. But they are trained from a very young age to develop remarkable skills in getting in and out of places secretly. So they are acrobats and climbers who can move in complete silence.

Most ninja come from Iga and Koga in the mountains, where they train in secret. They develop their physical agility and stamina with long runs, gymnastics, and swimming. They practice climbing and using fine ropes and rope ladders. And they become skilled in trickery and the use of weapons for silent assassination. Some say they dress in black—more often they are disguised as ordinary people!

## Sneaky Tactics

No one knows all the ninja's secret tricks. But they are amazing at hiding and surprise attacks: *tanuki-gakure* means hiding among tree foliage; *uzura-gakure* means curling up on the ground invisibly among leaf litter, like a quail; and *hitsuke* means starting a decoy fire.

Disguise: Ninja often dress and look exactly like ordinary peasants.

Kamuso Buddhist monks wear large basket hats—a perfect ninja disguise.

Underwater: A breathing tube allows ninja to hide underwater.

Weapons: A *noroshi* pot can be thrown or placed to fill the air with smoke.

A *fukiya* is a blowpipe that looks like a flute, but instead fires poison darts.

# INTO Battle

Today is October 17, 1561. *Aagh*, I am in my first battle—the terrible battle of Kawanakajima! The noise is appalling and I am fighting for my life! My daimyo joined with the great Takeda Shingen to fight against the forces of Uesugi Kenshin. We had a plan to encircle Kenshin's army. But Kenshin's men crept down on us in the night, wrapping their horses' hooves in cloth to silence them. Now we are battling them at close quarters. All my training never prepared me for the sheer ferocity and terror of it all. I must regain my haragei and fight like a true samurai. If not, I will soon be dead...

## The Big Fight

At the height of the battle, Uesugi Kenshin burst through to reach Takeda Shingen in the river and almost killed him, but Shingen just deflected his deadly blow. This was one of the most famous one-to-one combats between two great samurai warriors.

Just as it seemed all was lost for us, the force sent by one of our generals, Yamamoto Kansuke, to encircle the Uesugi, came hurtling down the hill and drove our enemy into the river. Fighting hard, the Uesugi retreated. We were too exhausted to pursue them.

# The Final Victory

To a samurai, the disgrace of defeat is worse than death. But you can win victory even in defeat by taking your own life. This is called *seppuku* or *hari-kiri*. It is the bravest thing a defeated samurai can do. It was our general Yamamoto Kansuke who devised the plan to encircle the Uesugi forces. In the midst of the battle, it seemed his plan had failed. So Kansuke charged against the Uesugi samurai alone and was hit by eighty bullets. Then he went on up the hill and killed himself, never knowing that his plan had won us the day in the end.

If I ever have to commit seppuku, I know how to do it. I will take a bath and put on a white kimono. I will lay my short wakizashi sword in front of me, write my farewell poem, and drink sake (rice wine). Then I will face death calmly.

## Last Words

The last thing a person facing death must do is write a short poem, whether he is committing seppuku, or dying naturally. At the moment of death we have a special insight into life. Just before the great samurai Toyotomo Hideyoshi died in 1598, he wrote this poem:

> *My life*
> *came like dew*
> *disappears like dew.*
> *All of Naniwa\**
> *is dream after dream.*

*\*Naniwa is an ancient site, that is now the city of Osaka.*

# Ten Shocking Samurai Facts

**1** Samurai often practiced their archery skills by shooting at dogs. The *inuomono* (dog-hunt) was their favorite training exercise.

**2** By tradition samurai were always right-handed.

**3** They used many different arrowheads. Some were hollow and whistled in the air to frighten their enemies!

**4** Swords were sacred, so swordmakers prayed and bathed before making a sword.

**5** When on patrol, samurai ate by cooking rice in their helmets.

**6** They burned incense in their helmets so that if anyone's head was cut off, it wouldn't smell bad. This, as with all aspects of cleanliness, was a point of honor.

**7** To test a sword, some samurai hung a dead enemy from a tree and tried making sixteen different cuts with it. Some were said to test them on live prisoners.

**8** One in every ten Japanese people was a samurai. So there may have been two million!

**9** English sailor William Adams, who was stranded in Japan in 1600, was one of the few foreigners ever to become a samurai. He was known as Miura Anjin.

**10** Samurai might have looked big in their armor. But they were mostly slim and only just about 5 feet (1.5 m) tall on average—tiny next to European knights.

# Glossary

**bushido:**
the way of the warrior, guiding the way a samurai lives

**daimyo:**
a Samurai overlord

**daisho:**
the pair of swords carried by a samurai

**haragei:**
willpower and inner strength

**jujutsu:**
the gentle art of hand-to-hand combat

**katana:**
the longer of the two swords typically carried by a samurai

**kenjutsu:**
the samurai art of swordsmanship

**kyujutsu:**
the samurai art of archery

**sensei:**
a Buddhist teacher

**shogun:**
warrior leader running Japan on behalf of the emperor

**tanegashima:**
early musket or hand cannon devised for use by samurai

**tessen:**
folding metal war fan used as a shield

**waka:**
a Japanese form of poem, often very short

**wakizashi:**
the shorter of the two swords typically carried by a samurai

# Index

armor, 22–23, 30
art of the bow, 16–17, 30

battle, 21, 26–27
bo-hiya, 21
bokken, 11
bows and arrows, 16–17, 21, 30
bushido, 12–13

calligraphy, 11

daimyo, 6, 8, 26
defeat, 28

fans, 18
female samurai, 16–17
flaming arrows, 21
foreign samurai, 30

guns, 20–21

hand-to-hand fighting, 18–19
helmets, 22, 23, 30

jujutsu, 18–19

kamae, 15
katana, 14, 15

Lady Tomoe, 17

naginata, 16
ninja, 24–25

place in society, 6
poetry, 11, 29

reading and writing, 11

samurai castles, 8–9
samurai schools, 10–11
seppuku, 28–29

shogun, 6, 7
swords, 14–15, 21, 28, 30

Takeda Katsuyori, 21
Takeda Shingen, 26
tanegashima, 20–21
tea ceremonies, 9
teachers, 13
*The Tale of the Heike*, 12

virtues, 12

wakizashi, 14, 23, 28
way of the warrior, 12–13
wooden swords, 11

## The Author

John Farndon is Royal Literary Fellow at Anglia Ruskin University in Cambridge, United Kingdom, and the author of a huge number of books for adults and children on science and nature, including international best-sellers. He has been shortlisted four times for the Royal Society's Young People's Book Prize.

## The Artist

Amerigo Pinelli lives in the heart of Naples, Italy. A long time ago, when he was a child, he met a pencil, and from that moment on he started to play, joke, fight, and make peace with it. He feels that living by doing the thing he enjoys most is a great gift. Three ladies make his life full of joy and color: Giulia, Chiara, and the latest arrival, Teresa!